NOEL C

Memoir Of A Great Actor

BY:

AMANDA GERALDINE

Table Of Contents

Preface

The English writer, composer, director, actor, and singer Sir Noel Peirce Coward (16 December 1899 - 26 March 1973) was praised for his humor, flamboyance, and sense of personal style, which Time magazine described as "a blend of humor and flair, stance and poise."

At the age of eleven, Coward made his professional stage debut while still a student at a London dance institution. He was first introduced to the upper society in which the majority of his plays would be set as a teenager. From his adolescence on, Coward enjoyed consistent success as a playwright, having more than 50 plays published. A large number of his plays, including Hay Fever, Private Lives, Design for Living, Present Laughter, and Blithe Spirit, are still performed regularly.

In addition to writing dozens of musical theater pieces, including the operetta Bitter Sweet and comedic revues, screenplays, poems, many collections of short stories, the novel Pomp and Circumstance, and a three-volume autobiography, he also wrote hundreds of songs. Coward acted and directed on stage and in films over six decades, appearing in many of his works as well as those of others.

Coward enlisted for military service at the start of the Second World War and took over the British propaganda headquarters in Paris. To leverage his influence to encourage the American people and government to support Britain, he also collaborated with the Secret Service. For his naval film play In Which We Serve, Coward received an Academy Honorary Award in 1943. In 1970, he was knighted.

He found new fame as a cabaret artist in the 1950s, singing his original songs like "Mad Dogs and Englishmen," "London Pride," and "I Went to a Marvelous Party."

Throughout the 1960s and 1970s, Coward's plays and songs had a surge in popularity, and his creations and aesthetics are still widely used today. Although he never came out, his homosexuality was openly explored by biographers, including Graham Payn, his longtime companion, and in posthumously published diaries and letters from Coward. In 2006, the former Albery Theatre in London, which was once known as the New Theatre, was renamed the Noel Coward Theatre in his honor.

Young Years

Teddington, Middlesex, a southwestern suburb of London, is where Coward was born in 1899. His parents were piano salesman Arthur Sabin Coward (1856–1937) and Violet Agnes Veitch Coward (1863–1954), a commander and surveyor in the Royal Navy. Coward's father lacked initiative and vigor, and the family's finances were frequently precarious. Early on, Coward caught the acting bug and, by the age of seven, was performing in amateur concerts. As a young child, he attended the Chapel Royal Choir School. Despite his lack of formal education, he was an avid reader.

Coward's first professional role was in the children's play The Goldfish in January 1911 as Prince Mussel, thanks to the encouragement of his aspirational mother, who sent him to a ballet school in London. In his first book of memoirs, Present Indicative, Coward penned the following:

A brief advertisement suddenly appeared in the Daily Mirror. A clever boy with a good appearance was needed, according to the ad, to feature in Miss Lila Field's production of The Goldfish, an all-kids fairy play. This appeared to put an end to all contention. I was a gifted boy, God knows, and I could pass for attractive after being cleaned up a bit. Miss Lila Field seemed to have no reason on earth not to grab me, and we both agreed that she would be a fool indeed to pass up such a fantastic opportunity.

He was given a role in the youth play Where the Rainbow Ends by the renowned actor-manager Charles Hawtrey, who the young Coward idolized and from whom he learned a great lot about the theater. In 1911 and 1912, Coward performed in the play at the Garrick Theatre in London's West End. In 1912, Coward also made appearances at the London Coliseum in Harold Owen's A Little Fowl Play, which starred Hawtrey, and at the Savoy Theatre in An Autumn Idyll (as a dancer in the ballet). In 1913, Coward was hired by Italia Conti to perform in the Liverpool Regional Theatre, and that same year, he was chosen to play the Lost Child Somewhat in Peter Pan. The next year, he returned to Peter Pan, and in 1915, he made another appearance in Where the Rainbow Ends. He also collaborated on some of his earliest plays with Esmé Wynne, Alfred Willmore, later known as Micheál Mac Liammóir, Fabia Drake, and Gertrude Lawrence, who, according to Coward in his memoirs, "gave me an orange and told me a few mildly dirty stories, and I loved her from then on." He also worked with Hermione Gingold, whose mother threatened to send "that naughty boy" out.

Early In His Teen Years

When Coward was fourteen years old in 1914, social painter Philip Streatfeild took him under his wing and most likely fell in love with him. Mr. Astley Cooper and her high-class acquaintances were introduced to him by Streatfeild. Streatfeild died in Rutland from tuberculosis in 1915, but Mrs. Astley Cooper continued to support her late friend's protege and welcomed him back to her estate, Hambleton Hall.

Coward continued to perform for the majority of the First World War, performing The Happy Family at the Prince of Wales Theatre in 1916 and Charley's Aunt on tour with Amy Brandon Thomas's company. He made an appearance in the Hawtrey-produced comedy The Saving Grace in 1917. According to Coward's memoirs, "Because of Hawtrey's love and care, my role was very significant and I did quite well in it. He put up with me for a very long time and taught me a lot of technical comic acting skills that I still use today over those two short weeks."

Coward enlisted in the Artists Rifles in 1918 but was deemed unfit for active duty due to a tubercular predisposition, thus he was medically released after nine months. He had an uncredited appearance in the D. W. Griffith movie Hearts of the World that same year. He started composing plays, working with his friend Esmé Wynne on the first two (Ida Collaborates (1917) and Ladies and Whiskey (1918)). The Rat Trap (1918), his first solo piece, was eventually performed at the Everyman Theatre in Hampstead in October 1926. He met Lorn McNaughtan during this time, who later became his secretary and held the position for more than forty years before she passed away.

Interwar Achievements

At the age of 20, Coward appeared in his light comedy, I'll Leave It to You, in 1920. After a three-week run in Manchester, his first full-length play in the West End premiered in London at the New Theatre (renamed the Noel Coward Theatre in 2006). Neville Cardus received grudging appreciation in The Manchester Guardian. Mixed yet hopeful reviews were received for the London production. Mr. Coward has a sense of humor, and if he can get past his propensity for smartness, he'll probably one day write a wonderful play, according to The Observer. The Times, on the other hand, praised the work enthusiastically, saying that it was "a fantastic piece of work from so young a head - spontaneous, light, yet always "brainy"."

Coward returned to performing in plays by other authors, starring as Ralph in The Knight of the Flaming Pestle in Birmingham and subsequently London. The play ran for a month (and was Coward's first play seen in America). I had a very, very long part, but I was very,

very awful at it, and I found Francis Beaumont and his former companion John Fletcher to be two of the dullest Elizabethan writers ever known." The Times dubbed the play "the jolliest thing in London," while The Manchester Guardian believed that Coward made the most of the character.

The Better Half, a one-act satire by Coward about a man's relationship with two women, was completed. In 1922, it had a brief run at The Little Theatre in London. The critic St. John Ervine said of the play, "Mr. Coward will write more intriguing plays than he now appears likely to write when he learns that tea-table chitter-chatter would better remain the domain of ladies."

Before a typescript of the play was discovered in 2007 in the archive of the Lord Chamberlain's Office, the official censor of theater plays in the UK until 1968, it was believed that the play had been lost.

Coward made his first journey to America in 1921 to attract American playwrights' attention. Despite his lack of success, he enjoyed the Broadway theater. Infusing its intelligence and energy into his work allowed him to achieve his first significant success as a playwright with The Young Idea. Following a regional run, the play premiered in London in 1923, with Coward playing one of the principal roles. The ratings were favorable: "It is exactly what Mr. Noel Coward refers to as a "comedy of youth" in his wonderful little farce. Youth also dominated the Savoy last night, cheering on everything with such fervor that you felt as though you were in the middle of a "rag," though not without excitement."

The play was praised by one critic more than Coward's newfound admirers, who noticed Bernard Shaw's impact on Coward's writing: "I was regrettably jammed in the middle of a group of his more effusive pals who welcomed each of his sallies with 'That's a Nolism!'"

From 1 February to 24 March 1923, the play was performed in London. Coward then switched to revues, co-writing and acting in André Charlot's London Calling!

With The Vortex, Coward experienced his first significant critical and commercial triumph as a playwright in 1924. A cocaine-dependent socialite and her nymphomaniac son are the subjects of the narrative (played by Coward). Some believed that using drugs was a way to hide their homosexuality; Kenneth Tynan later called it "a jeremiad against drugs with a speech that sounds today not so much awkward as high-heeled."

The Vortex's portrayal of drug usage and sexual vanity among the upper classes was considered disturbing in its day. Its fame and ferocious performances drew sizable audiences, which supported a transfer from a small suburban theater to a bigger one in the West End. Coward gathered the funds to create the play himself because he was still having problems finding producers. The American stockbroker Jack Wilson, who later worked as a director and producer, was introduced to Coward during the run of The Vortex. Wilson became both his manager and his lover. Wilson initially did a good job of managing Coward's business affairs but subsequently used his position to steal from his employer.

There was a huge demand for new Coward pieces as a result of the success of The Vortex in both London and America. He debuted Falling Angels in 1925, a three-act comedy that featured two middle-aged women who were slowly getting intoxicated while waiting for their shared boyfriend. The comedy pleased and surprised audiences. The first Coward play to secure a long-lasting spot in the canon of popular theater, Hay Fever, debuted in 1925 as well. In this comedy, four egotistical members of an artistic family casually invite friends to spend the weekend at their country home, where they bemuse and irritate each other's visitors. Some authors have noticed traces of Mrs. Astley Cooper, Coward's former mentor, and her milieu in the family's characters. The play gained notoriety in the 1970s and was hailed as a masterpiece by The Times as a "dazzling achievement; like The Importance of Being Earnest, it is pure comedy with no aim other than to amuse, and it depends only on the interplay of individuals, not on intricate comic machinery."

The Vortex, Fallen Angels, Hay Fever, and On with the Dance were the four plays that Coward had running on the West End by June 1925.

Coward was writing a lot of plays and acting in both his own and other people's. His fast-paced performance in The Constant Nymph soon caught up with him. After collapsing and being told to take a month off work, he disobeyed the doctor's orders and boarded a ship for the US to begin rehearsals for his play This Was a Man. He fell again in New York and had to take a long break, recovering in Hawaii.

Other Coward works produced in the mid-to late 1920s included the plays Easy Virtue (1926), a drama about a divorcee's conflict with her snobbish in-laws; The Queen Was in the Parlour (1926), a Ruritanian romance; This Was a Man (1926), a comedy about adulterous aristocrats; The Marquise (1927), an eighteenth-century costume drama; Home Chat (1927), a comedy (1928). None of these performances have been included in the standard repertoire, but the most recent one featured "A Room with a View," one of Coward's most well-known songs. During this time, Sirocco (1927), a drama about free love among the wealthy, was his biggest flop. Ivor Novello, who appeared in it, was described by Coward as "the two most beautiful things in the universe" along with "my mind." Theatergoers violently protested the play during curtain calls and spat at Coward as he exited the building.

"My first inclination was to leave England immediately," Coward later recalled of this failure, "but this seemed too craven a move, and also too satisfying to my opponents, whose numbers had by then swollen in our minds to nearly the entire population of the British Isles."

Coward was one of the highest-paid writers in the world by 1929, earning £50,000 per year, or more than $3 million in 2020 dollars. During the Great Depression,

Coward flourished, penning a string of hits. They included both small-scale comedy and elaborate spectacles. Examples of the former include the operetta Bitter Sweet (1929), which tells the story of a woman who marries her music teacher, and the historical extravaganza Cavalcade (1931) at Drury Lane, which covered the lives of two families for thirty years and required a sizable cast, enormous sets, and a sophisticated hydraulic stage. The best picture Oscar was awarded for the 1933 film adaptation of the book. Intimate hits by Coward during the time included Private Lives (1930) and Design for Living (1932).

Coward co-starred in Private Lives with the youthful Laurence Olivier and his most well-known stage companion, Gertrude Lawrence. Selling out in both London and New York was a career high point for both Coward and Lawrence. Because Coward detested long runs, he established a restriction that he may only appear in a play for three months at any given location. Written for Alfred Lunt and Lynn Fontanne, Design for Living was so obscene—with its topic of bisexuality and ménage à trois—that Coward gave it its New York debut knowing that it wouldn't make it through the censor in England.

Conversation Piece, an operetta that Coward wrote, produced and co-starred in both London and New York in 1933, starred the French soprano Yvonne Printemps (1933). Then, in Tonight at 8.30 (1936), a cycle of ten short plays performed in various combinations over three evenings, he wrote, directed, and co-starred with Lawrence.

Brief Encounter, a 1945 David Lean film, was based on one of these plays, Still Life. Tonight at 8.30 was followed by a revue called Set to Music and the 1938 musical Operette, whose most well-known piece is "The Stately Houses of England" (1938, a Broadway version of his 1932 London revue, Words, and Music). This Happy Breed, a drama about a working-class family, and Present Laughter, a comedic self-caricature with an egomaniacal actor as the main character, were Coward's final pieces before the war. Despite having both been written in 1939, these were both first performed in 1942.

Many of Coward's most well-known songs were recorded between 1929 and 1936 for His Master's Voice (HMV), and are now available again on CD. These songs include the sentimental "I'll See You Again" from Bitter Sweet, the lighthearted "Mad Dogs, and Englishmen" from Words and Music, and "Mrs. Worthington."

Second World War

Coward left the theater when the Second World War started and sought out official military employment. He worked for British intelligence after leading the British propaganda office in Paris, where he concluded that "if the policy of His Majesty's Government is to bore the Germans to death I don't think we have time." His mission was to use his notoriety to persuade the American public and government leaders to support aiding Britain. He was upset that the British press criticized him for traveling to another country while his fellow citizens suffered at home, but he was unable to admit that he was working for the Secret Service. Winston Churchill prevented King VI from bestowing Coward with a knighthood for his contributions in 1942. Churchill mentioned Coward's £200 fine for breaking currency laws in 1941 as justification for withholding the honor, keeping in mind how the public would see Coward's extravagant lifestyle.

Coward was slated to be detained and killed in The Black Book, along with other individuals like Virginia Woolf, Paul Robeson, Bertrand Russell, C. P. Snow, and H. G. Wells, had the Germans conquered Britain. During the war, when this was discovered, Coward wrote:

"I should have laughed if someone had told me at the time that I was quite high on the Nazi blacklist. One of the many persons who shared the honor with me was Rebecca West, and she sent me a telegram that said, "My beloved - the folks we should have been seen dead with."

Churchill believed that rather than gathering intelligence, Coward would be better suited to amuse the troops and the civilian population: "Go and sing to them when the cannons are firing - that's your job!" Coward took this advice despite being disappointed. Across Europe, Africa, Asia, and America, he continuously toured, performed, and sang. Popular songs with a war theme that he wrote and recorded include "London Pride" and "Don't Let's Be Beastly to the Germans."

German bombs destroyed his London home in 1941, so he temporarily moved to the Savoy Hotel. He joined Carroll Gibbons and Judy Campbell in an impromptu cabaret during one air raid on the Savoy's neighborhood to distract the imprisoned guests from their anxieties. The naval drama In Which We Serve was another wartime endeavor for Coward, who also served as co-director (with David Lean), performer, and composer. Both sides of the Atlantic enjoyed the movie, and at the 1943 Academy Awards ceremony, he received an honorary certificate of merit. Coward based his portrayal of a navy captain on his friend Lord Louis Mountbatten. Later, Lean would adapt three Coward plays for the big screen.

The immensely popular black comedy Blithe Spirit (1941), about a novelist who investigates the occult and employs a medium, is Coward's most enduring work from the war years. After his first wife's ghost returns during a séance, the novelist and his second wife are left in disarray. It was produced on Broadway as well, where its original run was 650 performances, and it broke box office records for a West End comedy with 1,997 straight performances. Lean directed a 1945 movie based on the play. In addition to his comedies Present Laughter and This Happy Breed, Coward performed on stage in 1942 in Blithe Spirit.

Coward made several offensive remarks in his Middle East Diary that many Americans found offensive. He specifically said that some of the mournful little Brooklyn boys who were "lying there in tears amid the alien corn with nothing worse than a bullet wound in the leg or a fractured arm" left him feeling unimpressed. The Foreign Office urged Coward not to travel to the US in January 1945 following objections from The New York Times and The Washington Post. Throughout the war, he did not visit America once more. Following the war, Coward created the alternate reality drama Peace In Our Time, which portrayed a Nazi-occupied England.

Subsequent Career

Coward's new plays produced after the war were somewhat popular but fell short of his pre-war hits in terms of audience appeal. Relative Values (1951) addresses the culture clash between an aristocratic English family and a Hollywood actress with matrimonial ambitions; South Sea Bubble (1951) is a political comedy set in a British colony; Quadrille (1952) is a drama about Victorian love and elopement; and Nude with Violin (1956, starring John Gielgud in London and Coward in New York) is a satire on modern art and critical pretension. Two musicals, Pacific 1860 (1946), a grandiose South Seas romance, and Ace of Clubs (1949), a show set in a nightclub, were commercial flops.

A review, Sigh No More (1945), was a mild success. The deaths of Coward's friends Charles Cochran and Gertrude Lawrence, in 1951 and 1952, respectively, were additional blows during this time. Despite his failures,

Coward maintained a high public profile; his 1953 performance as King Magnus in Shaw's The Apple Cart, in which Margaret Leighton also starred, received favorable press coverage, and his cabaret act, which he honed during his wartime tours entertaining the troops, was a smash hit both in London at the Café de Paris and later in Las Vegas. Kenneth Tynan, a critic for theater, stated:

You must see him in a cabaret to get a whole picture of his public and private selves. He padded down the famous stairs, stopped in front of the microphone while wearing black suede, raised both hands in a gesture of blessing, and then began to demonstrate how these things should be done. He gave us "I'll See You Again" and the other bat's-wing melodies of his childhood while baring his fangs as if revealing some monstrous edifice and cooing in a baritone.

Nothing he says or does at these times sounds forced or dry; his leathery, browned face still has an enthusiast's expression. Coward engages in careful romping if that is even conceivable. He doesn't owe much to earlier wits like

Labouchere or Wilde. Their best offerings must be given slowly, even sluggishly. Cowards show up with machine-gun-like staccato impulsivity.

Noel Coward at Las Vegas, a live recording of Coward's cabaret act from Las Vegas in 1955, was so popular that CBS hired Coward to write and direct a trilogy of three 90-minute television specials for the 1955–56 season. The first of these, Together With Music, featured Coward in several of the songs from his Las Vegas act and teamed him with Mary Martin. Then came the productions of This Happy Breed with Edna Best and Roger Moore, as well as Blithe Spirit, in which he co-starred with Claudette Colbert, Lauren Bacall, and Mildred Natwick. Despite rave reviews, the number of viewers was only average.

"Dad's Renaissance": Coward's popularity soared in the 1960s; on this poster, Al Hirschfeld's illustration of Coward is depicted rather than the actors who played the lead roles in this 1968 production.

Coward kept producing plays and musicals in the 1950s and 1960s. His 1953 adaptation of Lady Windermere's Fan, After the Ball, was his final West End musical to make its debut; his next two musicals both had their Broadway debuts. The most popular musical Coward wrote after World War II, Sail Away (1961), had performances in America, Britain, and Australia. It was set on an opulent cruise ship. The Sleeping Prince (1963) was the inspiration for the musical The Girl Who Came to Dinner, which lasted for just three months. High Spirits, a popular 1964 Broadway musical adaption of Blithe Spirit, was directed by him. Look After Lulu! (1959), a comedy, and Waiting in the Wings (1960), a tragi-comic depiction of old age, are two of Coward's latter pieces that were successful despite "critical scorn."

Coward stated that the main goal of a play should be to amuse the audience, and he avoided modernism because he thought it was boring for the public but exciting for the critics. More positive reviews were given to his humorous book Pomp and Circumstance (1960), which described life in a tropical British colony.

Suite in Three Keys (1966), a trilogy that was set in a hotel penthouse suite, was Coward's last theatrical hit. The line, "I would like to act once more before I fold my bedraggled wings," was written by him as his swan song as a theatrical performer. The trilogy received raving reviews and did well at the UK box office. Coward broke from his usual tact and played a homosexual character in one of the three plays, A Song at Twilight. Coward received fresh critical acclaim for the risky piece. He wanted to star in the trilogy on Broadway, but he couldn't go because of his health. Only two of the Suite in Three Keys plays—renamed Noel Coward in Two Keys and starring Hume Cronyn—were presented in New York.

Later in his career, with films like Around the World in 80 Days (1956), Our Man in Havana (1959), Bunny Lake Is Missing (1965), and Boom! (1968), and The Italian Job, Coward had a surge in popularity (1969). He declined stage and film opportunities in the 1950s, such as the chance to write a musical adaptation of Pygmalion (two years before My Fair Lady was written), the chance to play the king in the stage production of The King and I, and the chance to play Colonel Nicholson in the movie The Bridge on the River Kwai. He declined an offer to play the lead in the 1962 movie Dr. No, saying, "No, no, no, a thousand times, no." He declined the part of Humbert Humbert in Lolita that same year, stating that "At my period of life the film tale would be plausible if the 12-year-old heroine was a sweet little old lady."

Coward's popularity and reputation were restored in the middle of the 1960s and the beginning of the 1970s by successful productions of his 1920s and 1930s plays and new revues honoring his music, such as Oh, Coward! on Broadway and Cowardy Custard in London. This return was known as "Dad's Renaissance" by him. Private Lives received a successful revival in 1963, first in London and subsequently in New York.

"I am thrilled and flattered and frankly a little flabbergasted that the National Theatre should have had the curious perceptiveness to choose a very early play of mine and to give it a cast that could play the Albanian telephone directory,"

He wrote in 1964 after being asked to direct Hay Fever with Edith Evans at the National Theatre.

Additional manifestations of "Dad's Renaissance" included a 1968 Off-Broadway production of Private Lives at the Theatre de Lys, directed by Charles Nelson Reilly and starring Elaine Stritch, Lee Bowman, and Betsy von Furstenberg. The theater poster for the production included an Al Hirschfeld caricature of Coward rather than a picture of the play or its stars, even though Coward had a stellar cast. The drawing accurately depicts how Coward's reputation had evolved by the 1960s: rather than being viewed as the slick sophisticate of the 1930s, he was now regarded as the doyen of the theater. The New Statesman noted in a 1964 article "Who would have imagined that Noel Coward would become the venerable figure of British theater during the 1960s? He was talking to reporters about "Dad's Renaissance" one morning, and the next he was standing next to Forster, T. S. Eliot, and the OMs, clearly the greatest living playwright in England."

According to Time, "his best work, with its inspired inconsequentiality, seemed to exert charm, period, rather than just a charm of the 1960s."

Death And Respect

By the end of the 1960s, Coward had arteriosclerosis, and he had memory loss occasionally while performing Suite in Three Keys. He was similarly affected by this in his role in The Italian Job, and he quit acting right away. In 1970, Coward received a knighthood and was made a fellow of the Royal Society of Literature. In 1970, he was honored with a Tony Award for lifetime achievement. The University of Sussex conferred an honorary Doctor of Letters degree on him in 1972.

On March 26, 1973, at the age of 73, Coward passed away from heart failure at his Jamaican home, Firefly Estate. He was buried three days later on the crest of Firefly Hill, which has a view of the island's north coast. The Poet Laureate, John Betjeman, penned and read a poem in Coward's honor at a memorial ceremony that was conducted in St. Martin-in-the-Fields in London on May 29, 1973. John Gielgud and Laurence Olivier also performed poetry readings, and Yehudi Menuhin plays

Bach. The Queen Mother unveiled a memorial stone in Poets' Corner at Westminster Abbey on March 28, 1984. The Queen Mother responded, "I came because he was my friend," when Graham Payn thanked her for coming and introduced her as Coward's partner.

After substantial renovations, the Noel Coward Theatre in St. Martin's Lane, which had previously opened in 1903 as the New Theatre and later changed its name to the Albery, was renamed in his honor and reopened on 1 June 2006.

In 1998, the Queen Mother inaugurated a statue of Coward created by Angela Conner in the lobby of the Theatre Royal, Drury Lane. Also, there are sculptures of Coward on exhibit in New York and Jamaica, as well as a bust of him in the Teddington library, close to the area of his birth. At the National Theatre in London, a Coward exhibition was organized in 2008. The Museum of Performance & Design in San Francisco and the Academy of Motion Picture Arts and Sciences in Beverly Hills, California, later held the exhibition. An exhibition honoring Coward debuted at the Guildhall Art Gallery in the City of London in June 2021.

Private Life

Coward was homosexual, but in keeping with the custom of the time, this was never made known in public. A comment by the writer Kenneth Tynan from 1953 came very near to acknowledging Coward's sexuality:

"He played Somewhat in Peter Pan forty years ago, and you could argue that he has been completely in Peter Pan ever since. Like Gielgud, Rattigan, and the late Ivor Novello, he is a congenital bachelor and has not allowed his personal life to divert his focus from his job."

Coward was certain that his private affairs should not be discussed in public and considered that "any sexual actions when over-advertised" were offensive. Coward refused to publicly admit his sexual orientation even in the 1960s, joking that "there are still a few old ladies in Worthing who don't know." Despite his hesitation, he persuaded Cole Lesley, his secretary, to draft a candid biography once Coward was declared legally dead.

The most significant association that Coward had with Graham Payn, a South African stage and screen actor, started in the middle of the 1940s and persisted until Coward's death. In several of his London productions, Coward included Payn. A collection of Coward's diaries was eventually co-edited by Payn and Sheridan Morley and released in 1982. Other people with whom Coward had relationships included playwright Keith Winter, actors Alan Webb and Louis Hayward, his manager Jack Wilson, and composer Ned Rorem, who revealed information about their romance in his diary.

Prince George, Duke of Kent, and Coward were pals for 19 years, but biographers disagree as to whether their relationship was platonic. Despite Coward allegedly telling historian Michael Thornton that there had been "a little dalliance," Payn thought it was. After the duke passed away, Coward remarked, "I suddenly found that I loved him more than I knew."

Esmé Wynne-Tyson, an actress and author, was Coward's first partner and frequent correspondent. Gladys Calthrop created the sets and costumes for many of his plays. Coward also kept close friendships with actresses Gertrude Lawrence, Joyce Carey, and Judy Campbell. Marlene Dietrich was described as "his loyal and lifelong admirer."

He was well-liked and respected in his field for being compassionate and generous to people who were struggling. There are tales of how he subtly met the needs or settled the bills of former theater acquaintances who had no claim on him. Coward presided over the Actors Orphanage, which received funding from the entertainment industry, from 1934 to 1956. In that role, he became a friend of the orphanage's young charge, Peter Collinson. He adopted Collinson like a son and aided in his entry into the entertainment industry. Collinson asked Coward to take on a role in The Italian Job when he was a successful filmmaker. In the movie, Graham Payn also had a little part.

Coward bought Goldenhurst Farm in Aldington, Kent, in 1926, and lived there for the majority of the following 30 years, except when the military used it during the Second World War. It is a Grade II listed building of Grade II. Coward departed the UK in the 1950s for tax-related reasons and faced heavy newspaper criticism. He initially made his home in Bermuda, but then purchased residences in Jamaica and Switzerland (in the village of Les Avants, close to Montreux), where he lived out the rest of his days. He lived next to and knew people from other countries, such as Ian Fleming and his wife Ann in Jamaica, Joan Sutherland, David Niven, Richard Burton, and Elizabeth Taylor. The Flemings' wedding was seen by Coward, but his diaries document his irritation with their continual fighting.

Coward held conservative political beliefs, but they were not unwavering. He hated the Neville Chamberlain administration for its appeasement of Nazi Germany, and he and Winston Churchill had strong disagreements on the 1936 abdication issue. England doesn't want a Queen Cutie, Coward informed Churchill, although

Churchill supported Edward VIII's desire to wed "his cutie," Wallis Simpson. Coward despised plays that used propaganda:

Respect must be shown for the theater. It is a strangely enchanted home and a dream temple. It is categorically not and never will be, a dirty, dimly lighted drill hall acting as a temporary platform for political agitprop.

Although his own opinions occasionally came through in his plays, Cavalcade and This Happy Breed are both "overtly Conservative political dramas constructed in the Brechtian epic manner," in the words of playwright David Edgar. Coward was an atheist in terms of religion. Writing about his opinions, ***"Do I have faith in God? I am unable to answer either yes or no; to me, the answer is unknown."***

Coward used the diaeresis to spell his first name ("The dots over the 'e' in Noël weren't added by me. The words did. If not, it's Nool instead of Christmas! "). He was referred to as "Noel" in The Times, The Observer, and other modern newspapers and books because the press and many book publishers failed to follow suit.

Public Perception

Coward questioned, "Why am I expected to always wear a dressing gown, smoke cigarettes from a long holder, and say 'Darling, how wonderful'?" Coward's diligent development of a skillfully produced image held the key to the solution. He quickly developed a taste for the high life as a suburban boy who had been adopted by the upper classes: "I am determined to travel through life, first class."

In his other well-known plays, like Private Lives and Present Laughter, he adopted the trend. He first wore a dressing gown onstage in The Vortex. He is described by George Walden as a contemporary dandy.

The Independent made the following remarks about the 2008 National Theatre exhibition: "Both his elegant cigarette holder and well-known silk, polka-dot dressing gown appear to be from another period. But 2008 is turning out to be the year that Britain rediscovers its love for Noel Coward."

In an early press photo of him sitting up in bed holding a cigarette holder, he was described as looking like an advanced Chinese decadent in the final stages of dope. As soon as he found success, he started polishing the Coward image. Coward wrote shortly after that:

I started donning colored turtleneck jerseys, more for comfort than for style, and soon after, my evening paper informed me that I had started a trend. I think this was somewhat accurate; in any case, throughout the following months, I saw an increasing number of our seedier West-End chorus guys parade around London in them.

He immediately started to be more careful about going far with the flamboyance, telling Cecil Beaton to tone down his attire because "it's crucial not to give the people a way to make fun of you." Coward was content, nonetheless, to use his lifestyle to gain attention. He revealed to Time magazine in 1969, "I behaved erratically. I followed all of the instructions. a portion of the work." The time stated that Coward's greatest talent was "projecting a sense of personal style, a combination of cheek and chic, pose and poise," rather than writing, composing, acting, or directing.

Coward's mother was deaf, so Coward developed his staccato speaking style to help her hear what he was saying. It also helped him get rid of a slight lisp. This clipped diction is unique to Coward. According to Coward, his moniker "The Master" "started as a joke and became true." It was applied to him starting in the 1920s. When asked by a journalist why he was known as "The Master," Coward mocked it by saying, "Oh, you know - Jack of all trades, master of none." However, he was able to make light of his immodesty:

"I don't feel like I matter all that much to the world. On the other hand, I have a strong sense of my importance to myself."

When the Time interviewer expressed regret, "I'm hoping it hasn't been boring for you to participate in all these interviews for your 70th birthday and to respond to the same old questions about yourself," Coward retorted. "The topic captivates my interest."

Tasks And Public Appearances

Coward appeared in almost 70 stage performances and wrote more than 65 plays and musicals, though not all of them were performed or published. Coward and other screenwriters turned his plays and musicals into more than 20 movies, and he appeared in 17 of them as an actor.

Stage Works

Plays

Dan Rebellato categorizes the plays into early, middle, and late phases in a survey from 2005. The plays of the 1920s and 1930s are referred to as "the archetypal theatrical works of the years between World Wars I and II" by Jean Chothia in The Oxford Encyclopedia of British Literature (2006).

Hay Fever (1925), which "shows a highly theatrical family running rings around a bunch of staid outsiders," is regarded by Rebellato as representative of the early plays. Easy Virtue (1926), on the other hand, "brings the well-made play into the twentieth century."

A few people, including playwright Sean O'Casey, were offended by "the seeming triviality" and rich, flippant characters of Coward's plays, despite their widespread appeal, according to Chothia, "perhaps, especially because of the ease with which his sexually charged writing seemed to elude censorship."

According to Rebellato, Private Lives (1930), with its "evasion of moral judgment, and the blur of paradox and witticism," is the best of Coward's early plays.

After establishing himself through his early triumphs, Coward experimented with theatrical genres during the 1930s. The cycle of ten short plays Tonight at 8.30 (1935) and the historical epic Cavalcade (1931), both of which included a large cast and played to packed theaters, are difficult to resurrect due to the cost and "logistical challenges" of performing them. Throughout the 1930s, he continued to challenge social norms.

Design for Living (1932), with its bisexual triangle, had to have its US premiere since it was outside the purview of the British censor. The 1920s and 1930s plays by Noel Coward are noted for having women who are "unusually for the period, at least as self-assured as the men, and as prone to seethe with desire or wrath so that courting and the battle of the sexes are waged on strictly equal terms," according to Chothia.

Present Laughter, This Happy Breed, and Blithe Spirit are the most well-known plays during Coward's middle period, which encompassed the late 1930s and early 1940s. These plays are less experimental and have more conventional plots. The first and third of them are frequently reprised in Britain and the States. Coward performed them on tour throughout Britain during World War II.

Most people believe that Coward's plays from the late 1940s and early 1950s demonstrate a decrease in his theatrical flair. Although the theatrical and political worlds saw significant change during the century for which Noel stood as an indescribably English figure, Noel himself underwent very little change, according to Morley.

In the post-World War II plays Peace in Our Time and Nude with Violin, Chothis writes, "sentimentality and nostalgia, frequently lurking but usually kept in control in earlier works, were cloyingly evident, while his writing was back on form with the astringent Waiting in the Wings." Notwithstanding the positive reviews for his final pieces, Suite in Three Keys (1966), the Coward plays that most frequently repeated are Hay Fever, Private Lives, Design for Living, Present Laughter, and Blithe Spirit, which were written between 1925 and 1940.

Revues And Musicals

Between 1928 and 1963, Coward created the lyrics and music for eight full-length musicals. The first, which he referred to as an operetta, Bitter Sweet (1929), was by far the most popular. In 1929 and 1931, it had 697 performances on the West End. In his subsequent musical, Conversation Piece (1934), Noel Coward again picked a historical setting: Regency Brighton. Bitter Sweet was set in 19th-century Vienna and London. Although reviews were favorable, the run was cut short after 177 performances because the principal actress, Yvonne Printemps, had to quit the cast to keep a filming commitment. With a cast of more than fifty, the play has never undergone a professional revival in London.

Operette, a third historical-themed musical, closed after 133 performances due to poor ticket sales in 1938. It was "over-written and under-composed," with too much plot and not enough strong numbers, according to Coward's later assessment.

For his next large-scale production, Pacific 1860 (1946), he persisted in a romantic historical narrative. The success of the Rodgers and Hammerstein production Oklahoma!, which preceded Pacific 1860 at Drury Lane and ran there for 1,534 performances, served as a reminder of Coward's incapacity to adapt to changing public tastes. It ran for 129 performances. Although Coward enjoyed Oklahoma!, according to his friend and biographer Cole Lesley, he "did not learn from it and the change it had brought about, that the songs should in some way further the tale." Coward furthered this misstep, according to Lesley, by "getting to write one song, nothing anything to do with the plot, that was an incredible showstopper in every single show."

Coward attempted to be modern in Ace of Clubs (1949), which was set in a modern Soho nightclub. Coward wrote, "I am furious about Ace of Clubs not being a real smash and I have come to the conclusion that if they don't care for first-rate music, lyrics, dialogue, and performance they can stuff it up their collective arses and go and see (Ivor Novello's) King's Rhapsody."

Despite performing 211 performances, it performed better than its three predecessors. For After the Ball, he tried again but failed to use a romantic historical background (1954 - 188 performances). His most recent two musicals had Broadway premieres as opposed to London. The 1961 play Sail Away, which takes place on a contemporary cruise ship, had 167 performances in New York and 252 in London. The Girl Who Came to Dinner (1963), which Coward reverted to for his final and least popular musical, closed after 112 performances in New York and was never presented in England.

With André Charlot's revue London Calling!, which he wrote the majority of the songs and part of the sketches for, Coward made his first appearance. This was before The Vortex, a play he wrote the next year and produced in 1924, marked his first significant success as an actor and author. The Noel Coward Society's list of his most well-known songs includes only one song from the revue, "Parisian Pierrot," performed by Gertrude Lawrence. His other early revues, This Year of Grace

(1928) and On With the Dance (1925), were warmly received by the public and the press, and they featured several songs that have remained well-known, such as "Dance, Little Lady," "Poor Little Rich Girl," and "A Room With a View." Crazy About the Boy, Mad Dogs and Englishmen, Fantastic Party, and The Party's Over Now were among the songs featured in Words and Music (1932) and its Broadway counterpart Set to Music (1939).

Coward wrote his final original revue toward the end of World War II. Sigh No More, which later, I regret to say, turned out to be the best part of the revue, was the title he had come up with. With 213 performances in 1945–1946, it had a mediocre level of success. The show's songs "I Wonder What Happened to Him?," "Matelot," and "Nina" are some of the most well-known. Coward was consulted about but did not compile, two 1972 revues, Cowardy Custard in London (the title was chosen by Coward), and Oh, Coward! in New York, at the premiere of which he made his final public appearance. Both were anthologies of his songs from the 1920s to the 1960s.

Songs

Coward produced 300 song lyrics. According to performing data from the publishers and the Performing Rights Society, the Noel Coward Society's website lists "Mad About the Boy" (from Words and Music) as Coward's most well-known song, followed by:

- I'll run into you soon (BitterSweet).
- In "Mad Dogs and Englishmen" (Words and Music).
- If Love Were Everything (BitterSweet).
- "I'll find you sometime" (Private Lives).
- I'll go after my hidden heart (Conversation Piece).
- The "London Pride" (1941).
- In "A Room With a View" (This Year of Grace).
- A "Mrs. Worthington" (1934).
- On with the Dancing, "Poor Little Wealthy Girl," and "The Stately Houses of England" (Operette).

Despite not being a fan of Gilbert and Sullivan's music, Coward's songwriting was greatly affected by it. He remembered:

"I came of age during a time when people still took light music seriously. Gilbert and Sullivan's words and melodies were hummed and strummed into my awareness at a young age. My relatives and uncles, who were numerous, would sing them singly and in unison at the least provocation. My father sang them, my mother played them."

According to his colleague Terence Rattigan, Coward was "the best of his kind since W. S. Gilbert" in terms of lyric writing.

Crucial Legacy And Reputation

According to playwright John Osborne, "His creation and contribution to this century is Mr. Coward. Those who are unable to see it should stay far away from the theater." Even the youngest among us will understand exactly what we mean by "a very Noel Coward sort of person," Tynan predicted in 1964. As a tribute on the occasion of Coward's seventieth birthday, Lord Mountbatten praised the flexibility of Coward and stated:

There are probably more painters than Noel, more novelists than Noel, more librettists than Noel, more musicians than Noel, more comedic actors than Noel, more tragic actors than Noel, more stage producers than Noel, more film directors than Noel, more cabaret performers than Noel, and more TV stars than Noel. If so, there are fourteen separate individuals present. The Master was the only person who integrated all fourteen separate designations.

The first generation of reviewers to recognize that Coward's plays would experience more than fleeting popularity was Tynan's.

They were "written in the most topical and perishable fashion imaginable, the cream in them turning sour overnight," Cyril Connolly claimed in the 1930s.

In the 1950s, what was considered daring in the 1920s and 1930s was seen as out-of-date, and Coward was never able to replicate the success of his pre-war plays. By the 1960s, reviewers had started to notice that Coward's best plays also dealt with recognizable characters and familiar relationships, with an emotional depth and pathos that had been frequently ignored, beneath the clever banter and the Art Deco glamor of the interwar years.

By the time of his passing, The Times had praised him, saying that "None of the great personalities of English drama has been more versatile than he," and that his plays were in "the classical lineage of Congreve,

Sheridan, Wilde, and Shaw." Shakespeare came out on top, followed by Coward in second place, in what The Stage referred to as a "millennium poll" of its readers to determine the theater, variety, television, or film professionals who have most influenced British culture.

A symposium published in 1999 to mark the centenary of Coward's birth listed some of his major productions scheduled for the year in Britain and North America, including Ace of Clubs, After the Ball, Blithe Spirit, Cavalcade, Easy Virtue, Hay Fever, Present Laughter, Private Lives, Sail Away, A Song at Twilight, The Young Idea and Waiting in the Wings, with stars including Lauren Bacall, Rosemary Harris, Ian McKellen, Corin Redgrave, Vanessa Redgrave, and Elaine Stritch. Hugh Wooldridge's centenary celebration, which featured more than 30 A-list actors and raised money for the Actors' Orphanage, was performed at the Savoy Theatre on December 12, 1999.

The Divine Comedy, Elton John, Valerie Masterson, Paul McCartney, Michael Nyman, Pet Shop Boys, Vic Reeves,

Sting, Joan Sutherland, Robbie Williams, and others have all recorded several of Coward's songs. Tim Rice once said of Coward's songs, "The wit and wisdom of Noel Coward's lyrics will be as lively and contemporary in 100 years as they are today."

Coward's songs, writings, distinctive voice, and mannerisms have all been widely mocked and mimicked, as seen in films like Privates on Parade, Round the Horne, and Monty Python. The actor Daniel Massey played Coward in the 1968 Julie Andrews film Star!, the BBC sitcom Goodnight Sweetheart, and a BBC Radio 4 series written by Marcy Kahan in which Coward was dramatized as a detective in the episodes Design For Murder (2000), A Bullet at Balmain's (2003), and Death at the Desert Inn (2005) and as a spy in the episodes Blithe Spy (2002) and Our M.O. The Broadway drama The Man Who Came to Dinner from 1939 included Beverly Carlton, one of many Coward-inspired characters.

Lunch with Marlene, a play by Chris Burgess about Coward and Dietrich's friendship, was performed at the New End Theatre in 2008. A musical revue featuring

Coward songs like "Don't Let's Be Beastly to the Germans" is featured in the second act.

Coward supported Harold Pinter's film adaptation of The Caretaker with a £1,000 investment since he was an early fan of Pinter's plays. Coward's influence has been noted by several critics in some of Pinter's plays. Tynan contrasted Coward's "stylized dialogue" to Pinter's "elliptical pattern." In 1976, Pinter paid it back by directing the National Theatre's production of Blithe Spirit.

Printed in Great Britain
by Amazon